DEAN LEWIS
A PLACE WE KNEW

PIANO
VOCAL
GUITAR

ISBN: 978-1-5400-5603-0

Visit Hal Leonard Online at
www.halleonard.com

Contact us:
Hal Leonard
7777 West Bluemound Road
Milwaukee, WI 53213
Email: info@halleonard.com

In Europe, contact:
Hal Leonard Europe Limited
42 Wigmore Street
Marylebone, London, W1U 2RN
Email: info@halleonardeurope.com

In Australia, contact:
Hal Leonard Australia Pty. Ltd.
4 Lentara Court
Cheltenham, Victoria, 3192 Australia
Email: info@halleonard.com.au

HOLD OF ME

Words and Music by
DEAN LEWIS

Driving beat

Walk - ing __ slow - ly, try'n' to find a place to __ go.

You be - gin to talk a - bout your __ ex, __ and the way that he would

lose con - trol. And all your friends are try'n' to __ throw __

___ me; they're ask - ing ques-tions I don't ___ know.   But ba-by, I would

buy   you ___ drinks ___ too, but I don't think you need   no ___ more.

Then you said, "I need noth - in' ___   from no - bod -

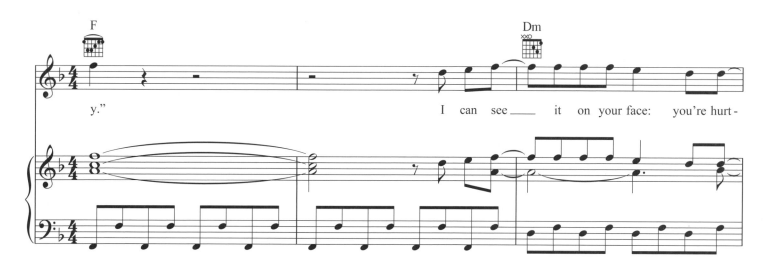

y."   I can see ___ it on your face: you're hurt -

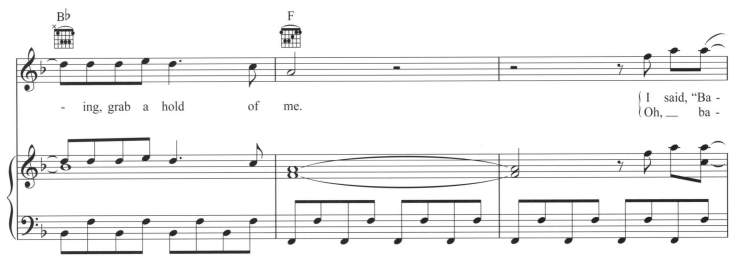

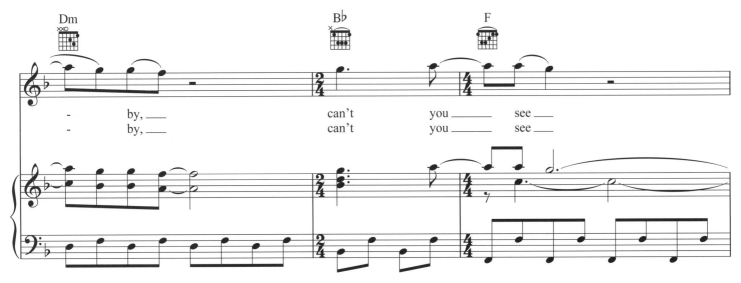

Oh, oh. _____ 'Cause your past __

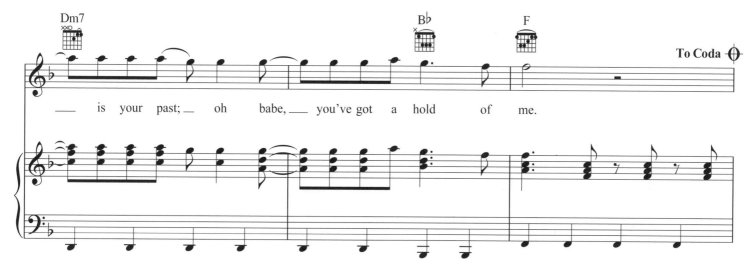

__ is your past; __ oh babe, __ you've got a hold of me.

I'm try'n' to fig-ure you __ out _____ as your're star-ing straight

back at __ me. And you tell me you don't like your __ fa-

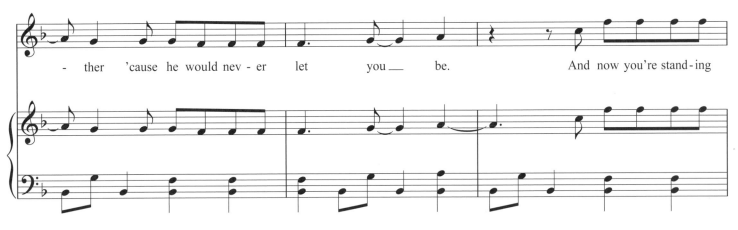

-ther 'cause he would nev - er let you __ be. And now you're stand-ing

be - side __ the win - dow; you're cov-ered in the light from __ the street. __

__ And I say that it __ gets cold __ here __ in win -

D.S. al Coda

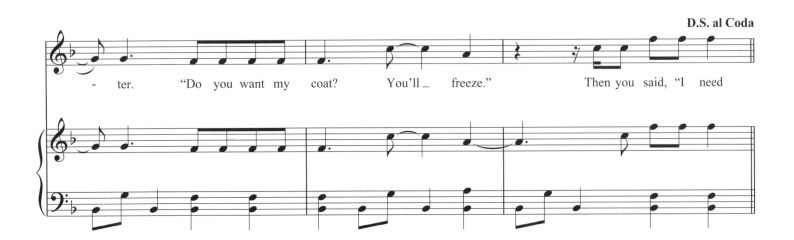

- ter. "Do you want my coat? You'll __ freeze." Then you said, "I need

-ing, grab a hold of me. I ____ said,

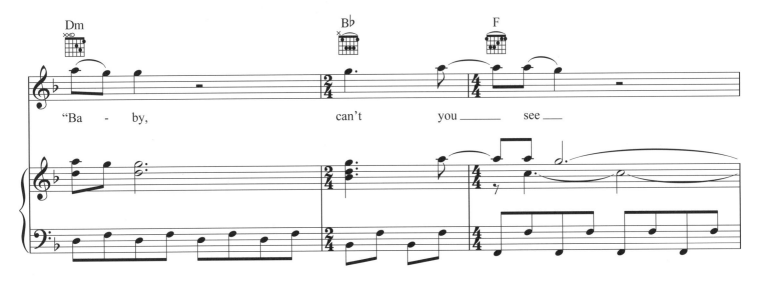

"Ba - by, can't you ____ see ____

that your past ____ is your past? Oh babe, ____ you've got a hold of

me." You've got a hold ____ of me.

Oh, oh. _____ 'Cause your past _

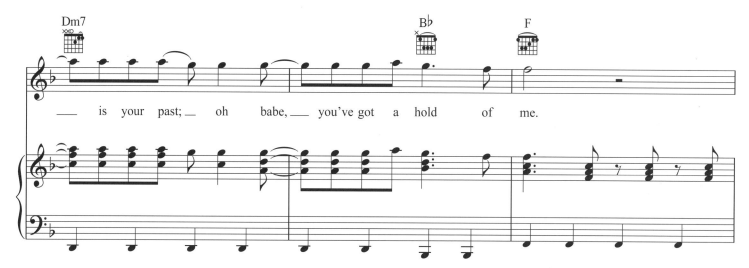

_____ is your past; _ oh babe, _ you've got a hold of me.

Oh, oh. _____

Oh, oh. _____   Oh oh. _____

7 MINUTES

Words and Music by DEAN LEWIS,
NICK ATKINSON and EDD HOLLOWAY

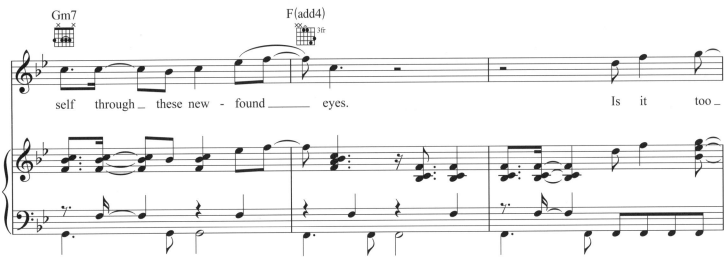

self through _ these new - found _____ eyes. Is it too _

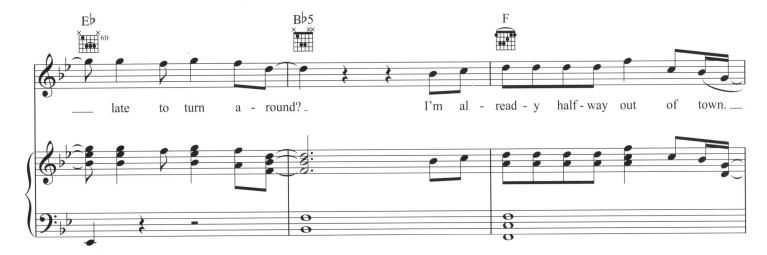

_ late to turn a - round? _ I'm al - read - y half - way out of town. _

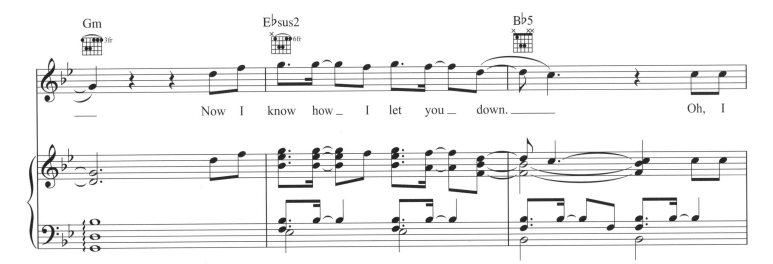

_ Now I know how _ I let you _ down. _____ Oh, I

fi - nal - ly fig - ured it out: I for - got to love you, love you,

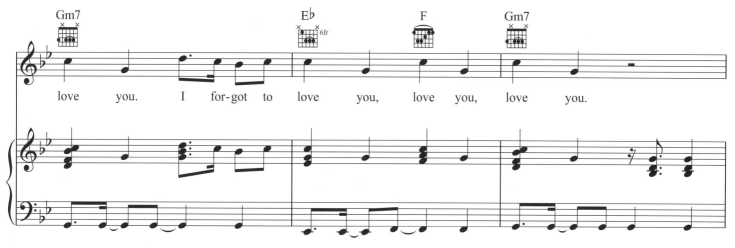

love you. I for-got to love you, love you, love you.

Ra - di - o's play-ing songs ___ for me and you. ___ "Chas-ing Cars" ___

___ re - minds ___ me of ___ nights in your room, drink - ing

wine un - der your win - dow, back when love was so damn sim - ple. How the

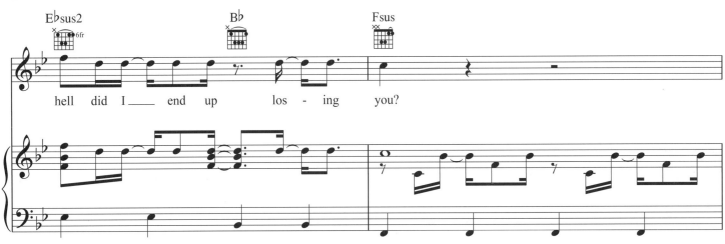

hell did I _____ end up los - ing you?

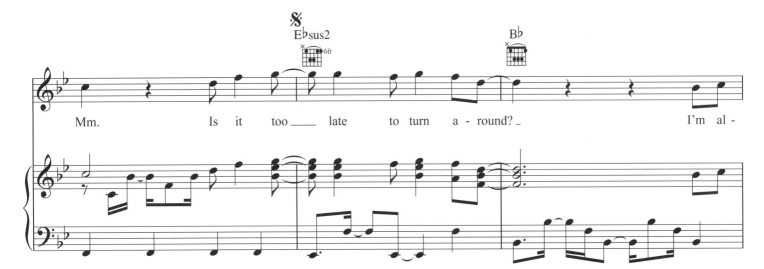

Mm. _____ Is it too _____ late to turn a - round? _____ I'm al -

read - y half - way out of town. _____ Now I

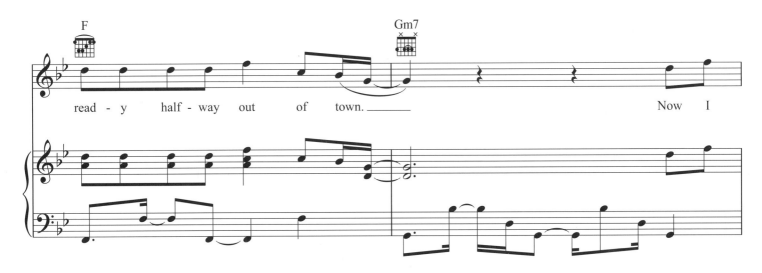

know how _ I let you _ down. _____ Oh, I

fi-nal-ly fig-ured it out: I for-got to love you, love you,

love you. I for-got to love you, love you, love you. I for-got to

love you, love you, love you. I for-got to love you, love you.

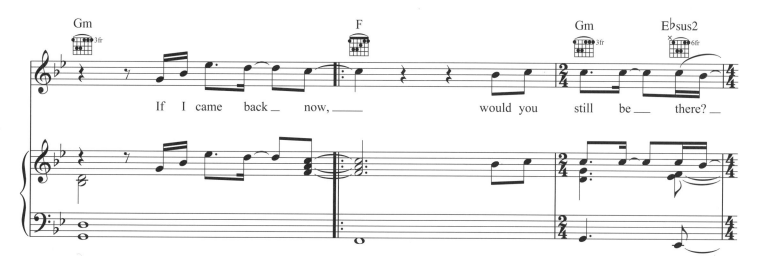

If I came back _ now, _____ would you still be _ there? _

STAY AWAKE

Words and Music by DEAN LEWIS,
STEVEN SOLOMON and NEIL ORMANDY

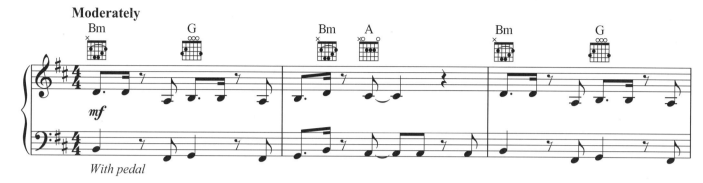

Trac-ing our fin-gers from right to left, __ we're

too drunk to e - ven walk. __

And all of a sud-den, you bring up our prob-lems, so I guess you wan - na

talk. _____ 'Cause they say, "The

big-ger the love, __ the hard-er the fall." ____ Well, I'm crash-ing through __ the

floor. __ Said you're leav - ing __

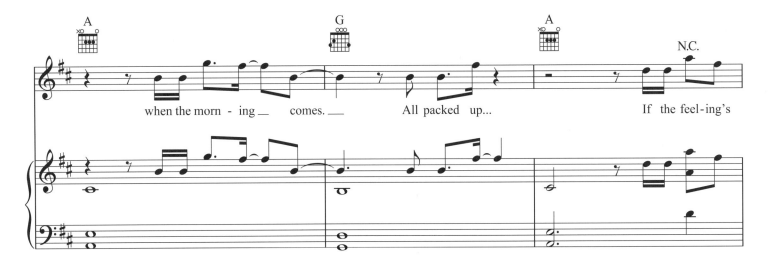

when the morn - ing __ comes. __ All packed up... If the feel-ing's

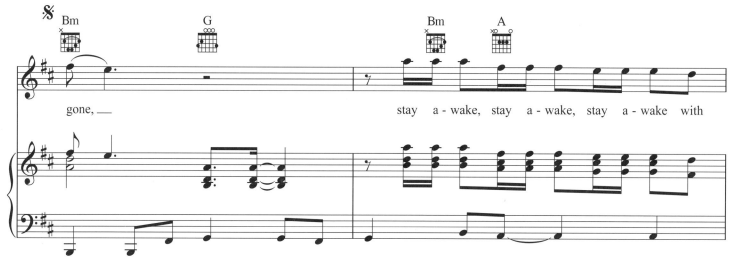

gone, ___ stay a-wake, stay a-wake, stay a-wake with

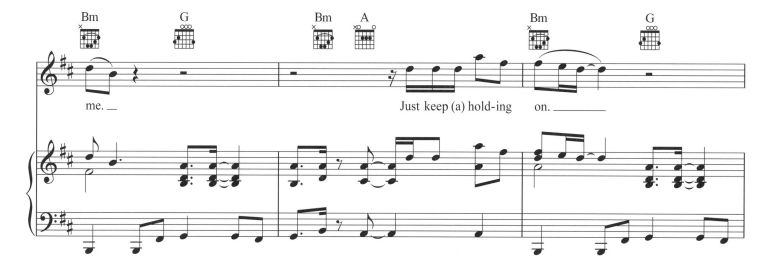

me. ___ Just keep (a) hold-ing on. _____

To Coda ⊕

Stay a-wake, stay a-wake, stay a-wake with me. ___

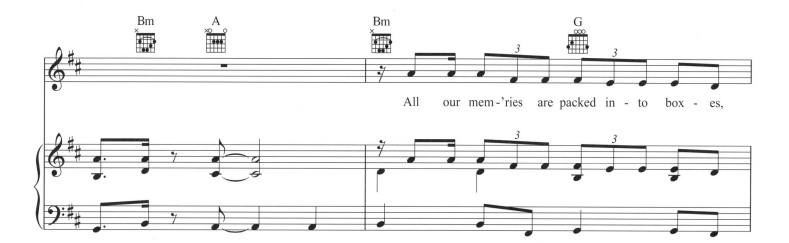

All our mem-'ries are packed in-to box-es,

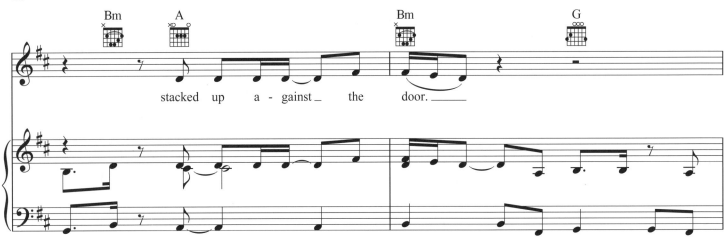

stacked up a - gainst __ the door. ____

'Cause they say, "The big - ger the love, _ the hard - er the fall." ___ Well,

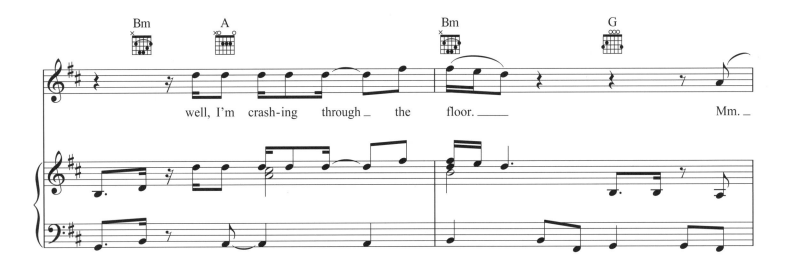

well, well, I'm crash - ing through _ the floor. ____ Mm. _

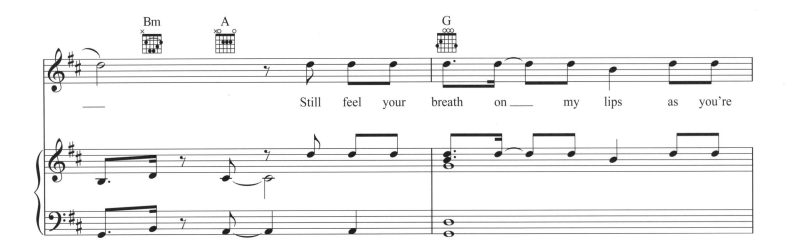

___ Still feel your breath on ___ my lips as you're

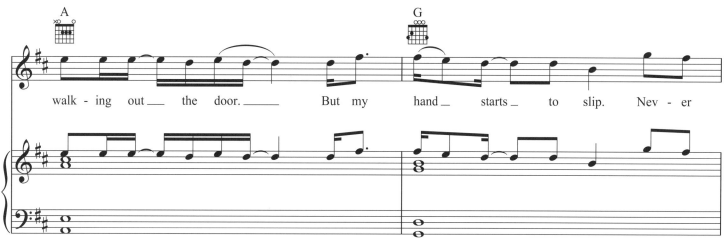

walk-ing out ___ the door. _____ But my hand ___ starts ___ to slip. Nev- er

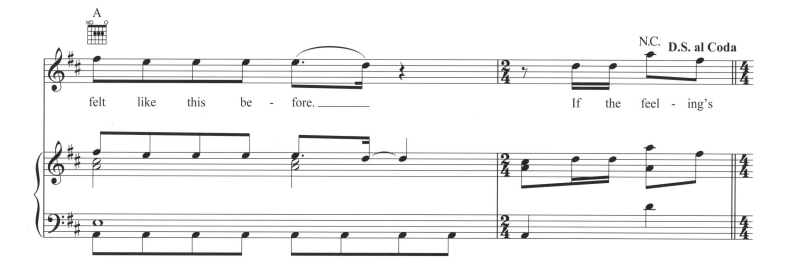

felt like this be - fore. _____ If the feel - ing's

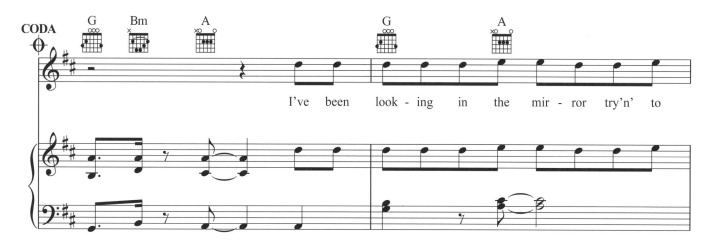

I've been look-ing in the mir-ror try'n' to

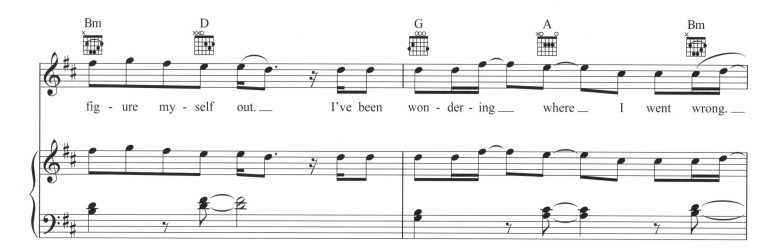

fig - ure my-self out. ___ I've been won-der-ing ___ where ___ I went wrong. ___

But now you're not here, __ it's like the day - light nev-er comes. __ So I'll

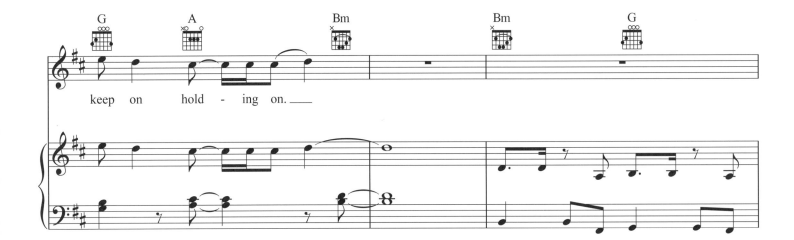

keep on hold - ing on. __

Said you're leav - ing __ when the morn - ing __ comes. __

__ All packed up... If the feel-ing's gone, __

stay a-wake, stay a-wake, stay a-wake with me. ___

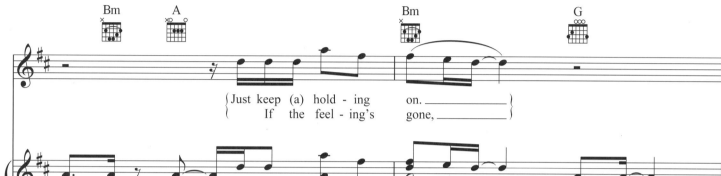

{ Just keep (a) hold - ing on. ____
{ If the feel - ing's gone, ____

Stay a-wake, stay a-wake, stay a-wake with me. ___

If the feel-ing's gone, _

A PLACE WE KNEW

Words and Music by
DEAN LEWIS

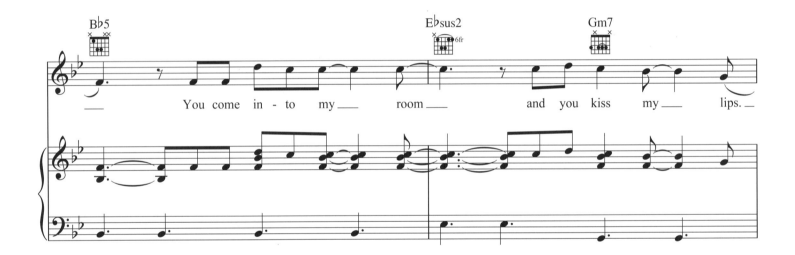

Recorded a half step higher.

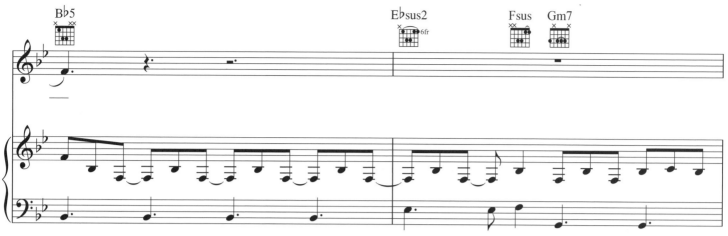

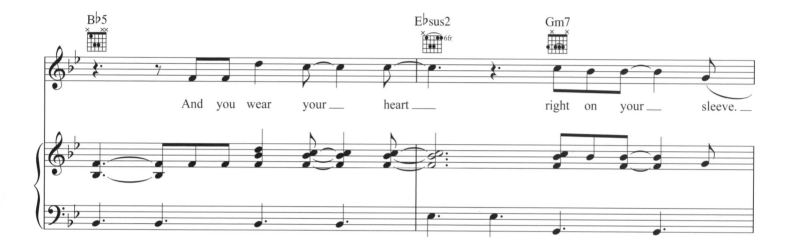

And you wear your ___ heart ____ right on your ___ sleeve. ___

___ but it took you a while to o-pen up to me. ___

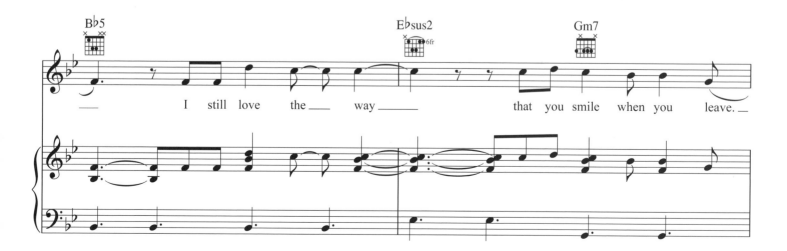

___ I still love the ___ way _____ that you smile when you leave. ___

And I know you get scared ___ when I'm a-way ___

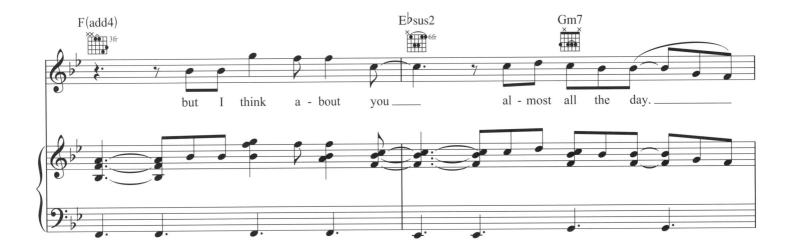

but I think a-bout you ___ al-most all the day. ___

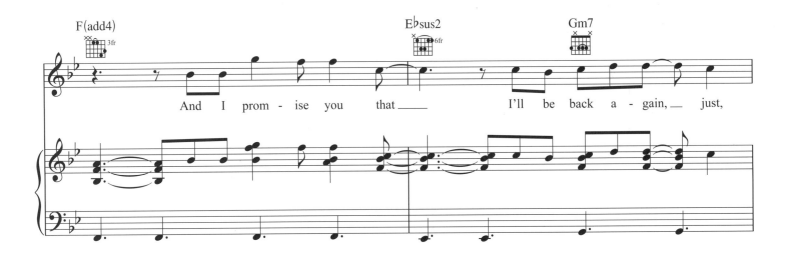

And I prom-ise you that ___ I'll be back a-gain, ___ just,

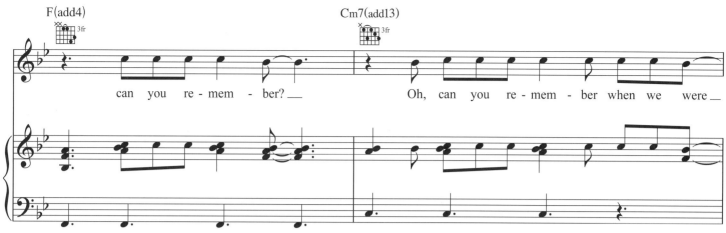

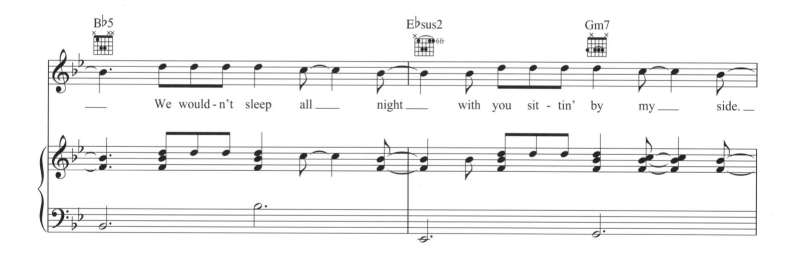

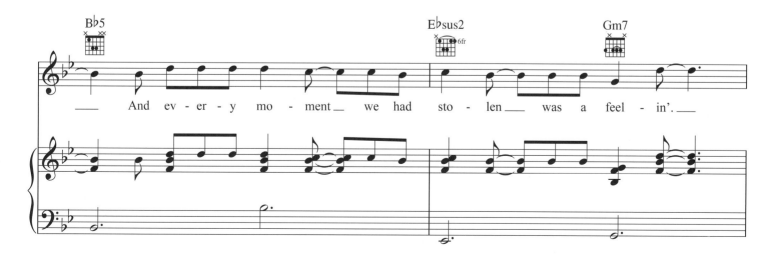

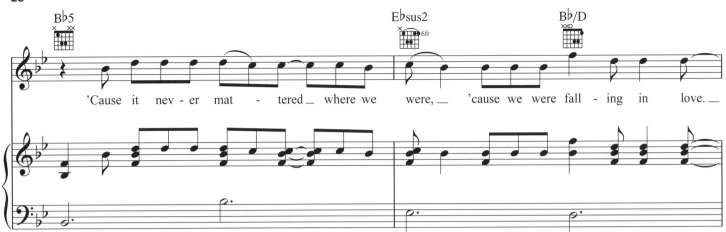

'Cause it nev-er mat - tered__ where we were,__ 'cause we were fall-ing in love.__

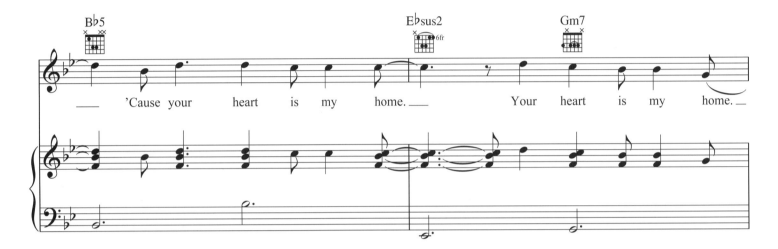

__ 'Cause your heart is my home.__ Your heart is my home.__

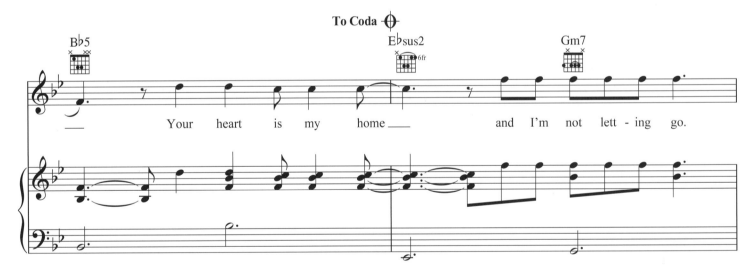

To Coda ⊕

__ Your heart is my home __ and I'm not let-ting go.

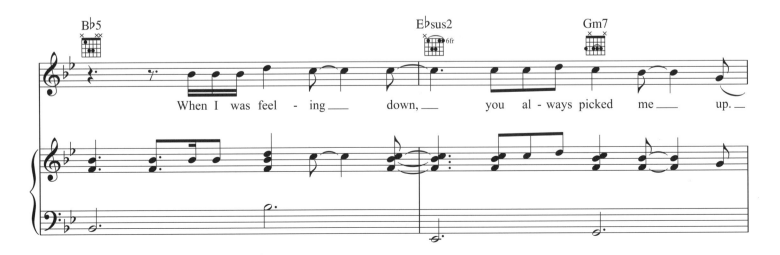

When I was feel-ing__ down,__ you al-ways picked me__ up.__

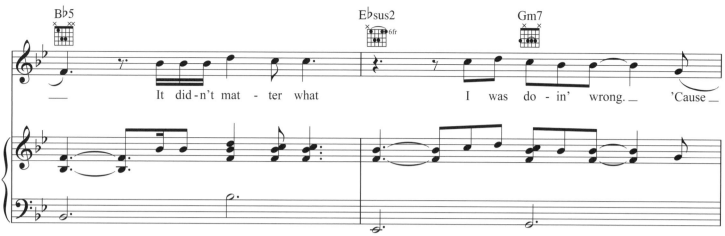

It did-n't mat - ter what I was do-in' wrong. ___ 'Cause ___

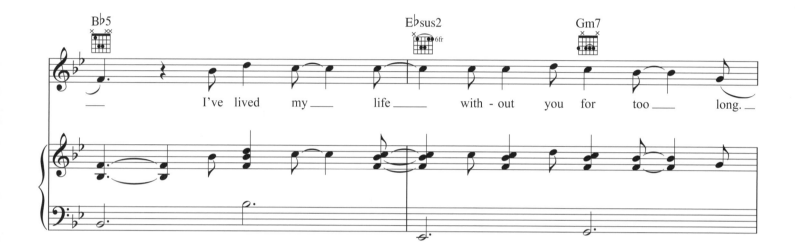

___ I've lived my ___ life ___ with - out you for too ___ long. ___

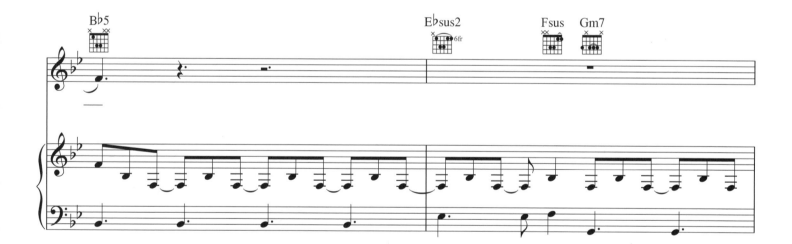

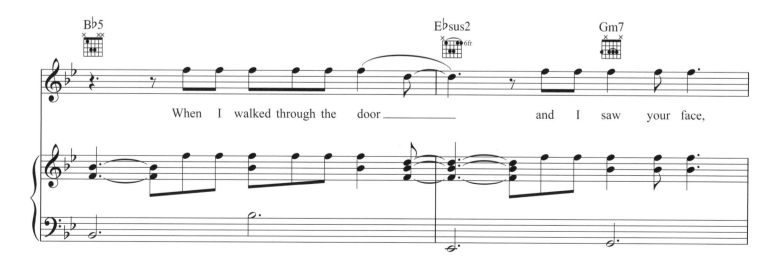

When I walked through the door _____ and I saw your face,

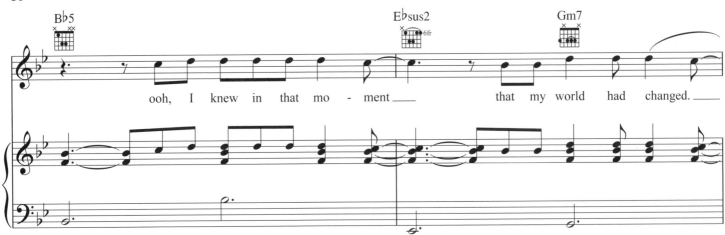

ooh, I knew in that mo - ment ___ that my world had changed. ___

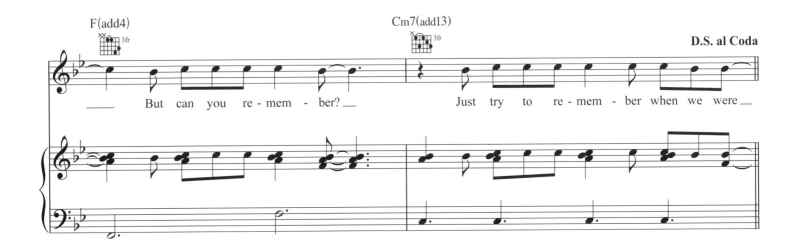

___ How can I live my ___ life ___ since you've been and ___ gone? ___

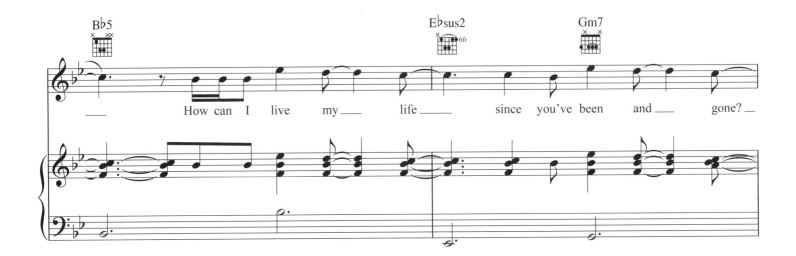

___ But can you re - mem - ber? ___ Just try to re - mem - ber when we were ___

___ and I'm not let - ting go, but at an - y ___ sin - gle mo - ment you ___ can

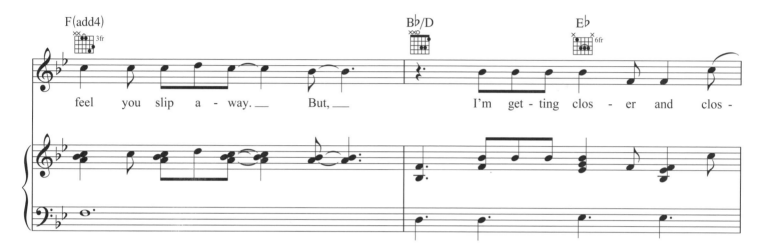

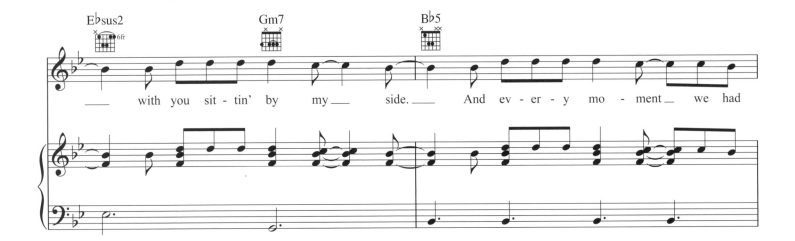

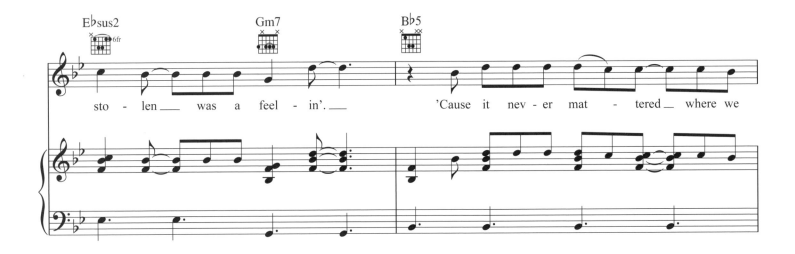

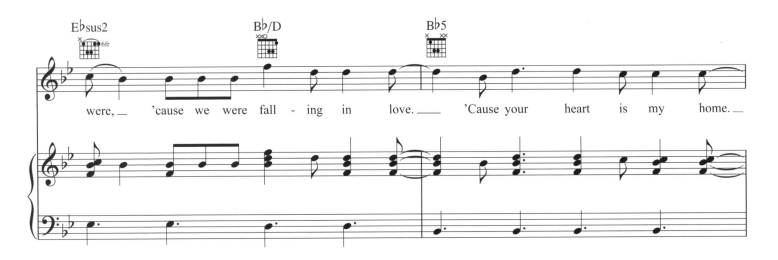

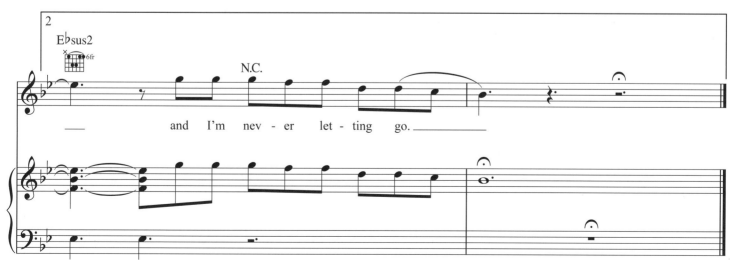

WAVES

Words and Music by DEAN LEWIS,
NICK ATKINSON and EDD HOLLOWAY

Fast Rock

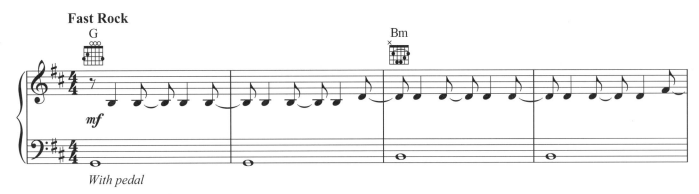

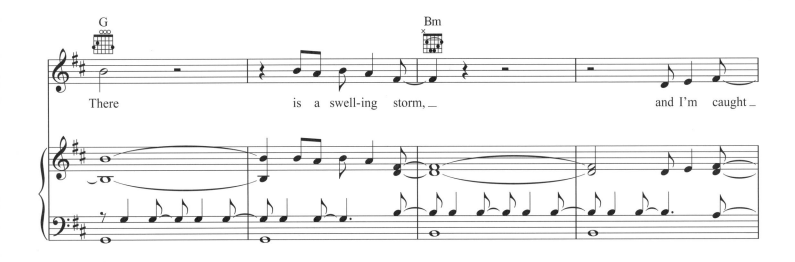

There is a swell-ing storm, ___ and I'm caught ___

___ up in ___ the mid - dle of ___ it all. ___

And it takes _____ con - trol _____ of the

per - son that __ I thought __ I was, __ the boy I used __ to know. __

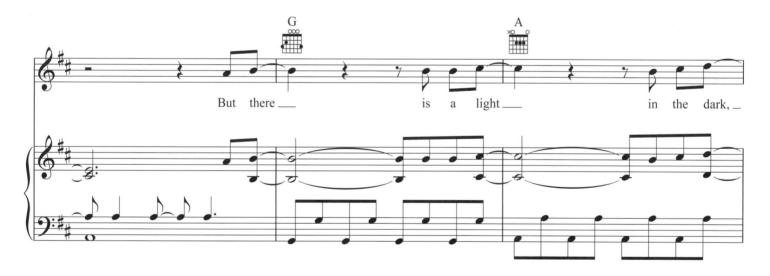

But there ___ is a light ___ in the dark, __

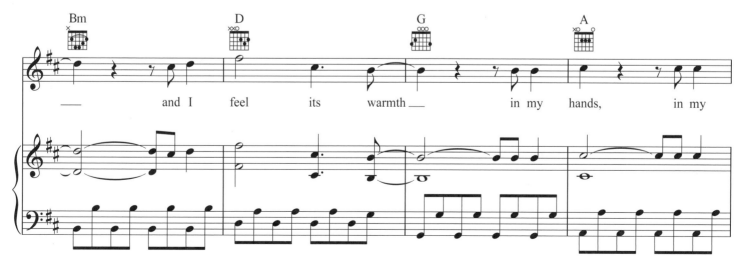

and I feel its warmth ___ in my hands, in my

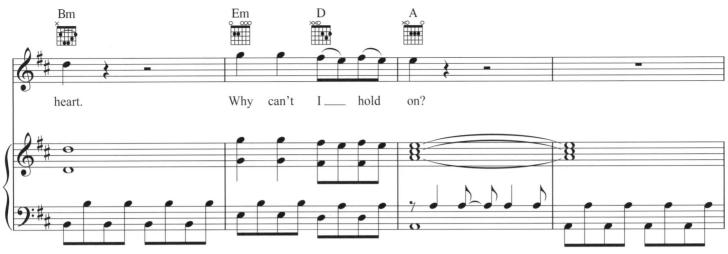

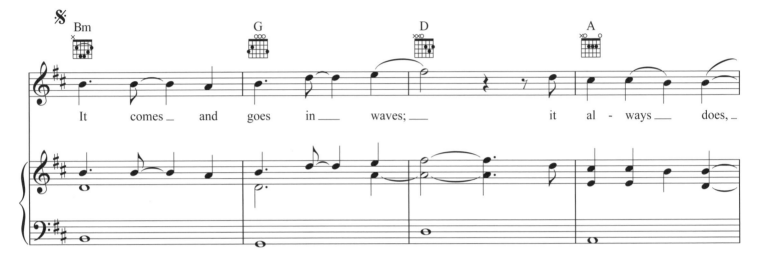

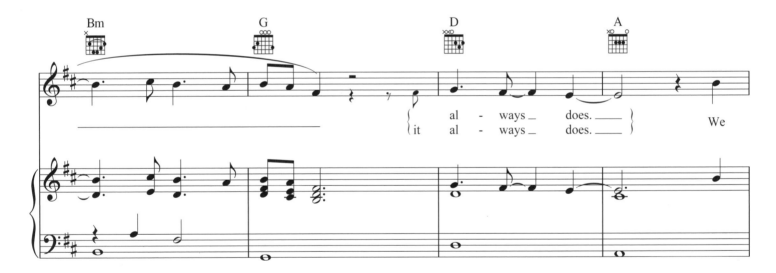

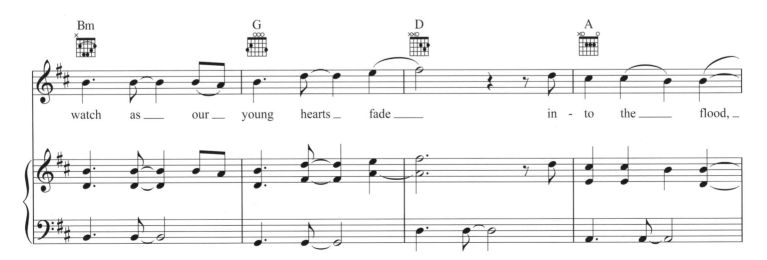

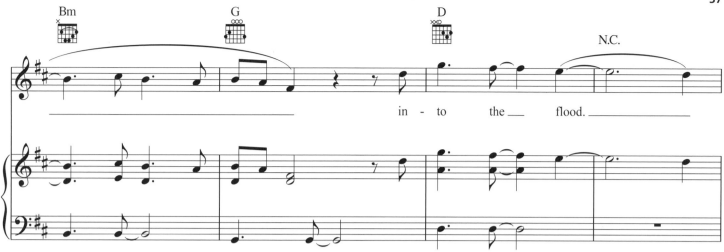

in - to the ___ flood. _____

And the free - dom of fall - ing, a feel - ing I

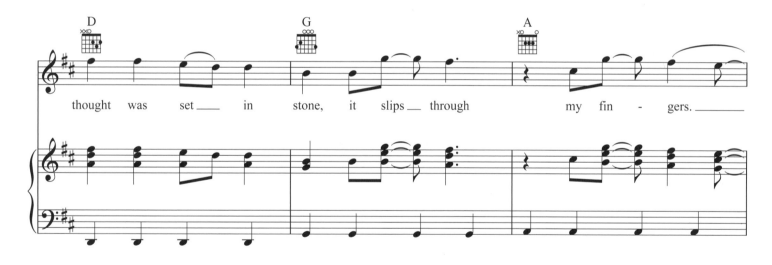

thought was set ___ in stone, it slips ___ through my fin - gers. _____

___ I'm try-ing hard ___ to let ___ go. It comes ___ and goes in ___ waves. _

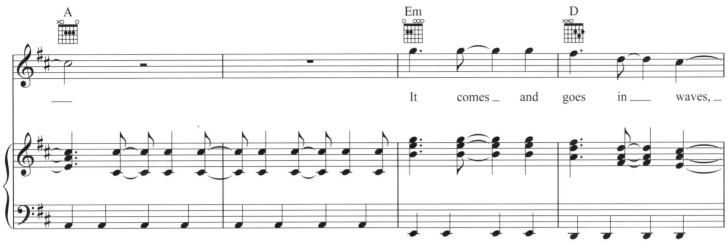

It comes — and goes in — waves, —

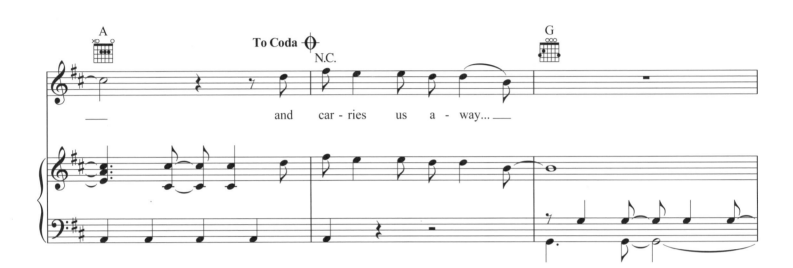

and car - ries us a - way... —

through — the wind, — down to — the place —

— we used — to lay — when we — were kids. —

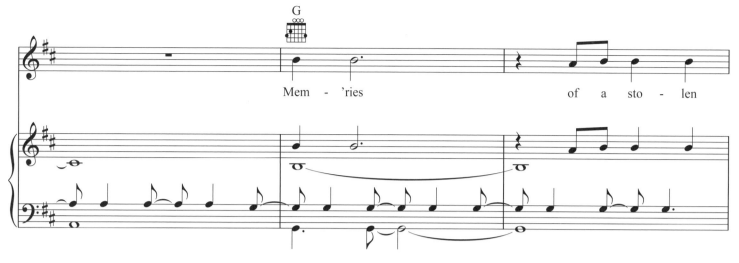

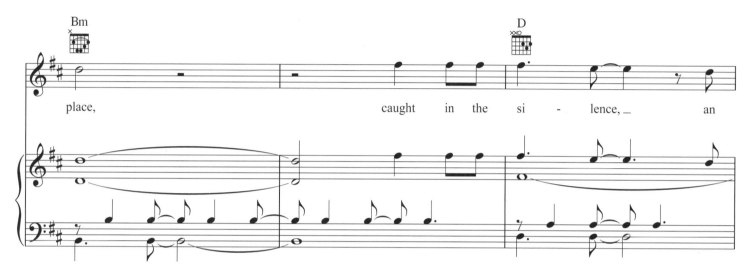

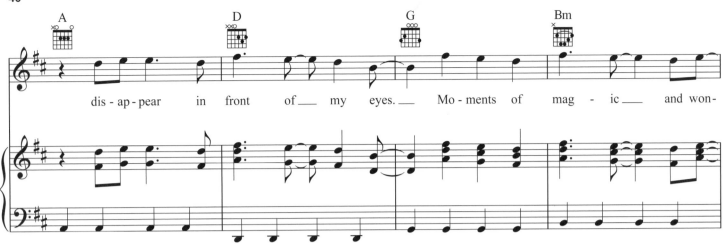

dis-ap-pear in front of __ my eyes. __ Mo-ments of mag-ic __ and won-

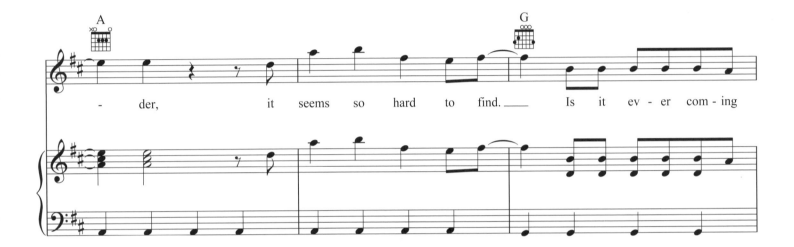

-der, it seems so hard to find. __ Is it ev-er com-ing

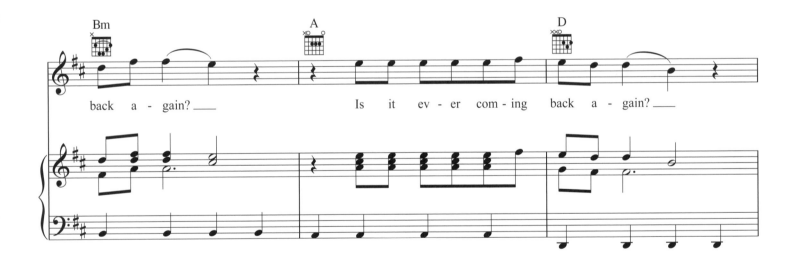

back a-gain? __ Is it ev-er com-ing back a-gain? __

Take me back to the feel-ing when ev-'ry-thing was left be-hind. __

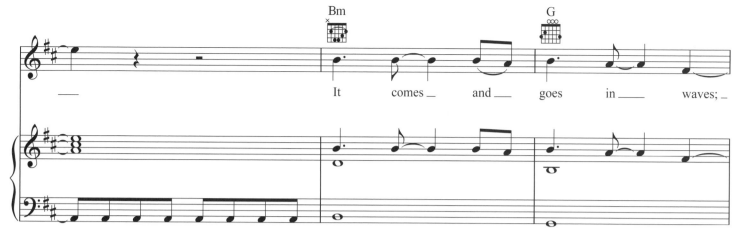

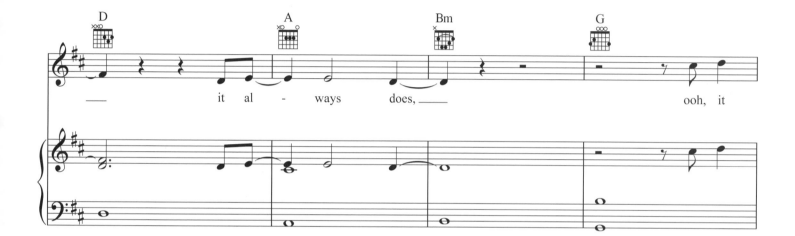

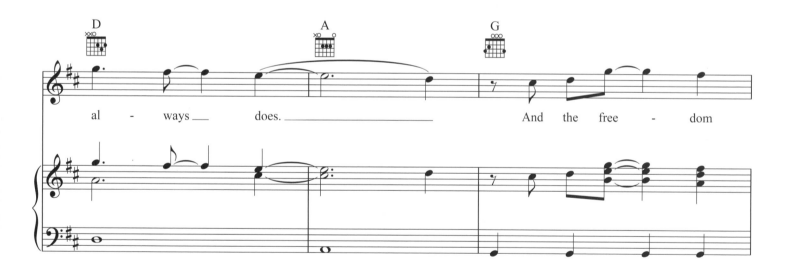

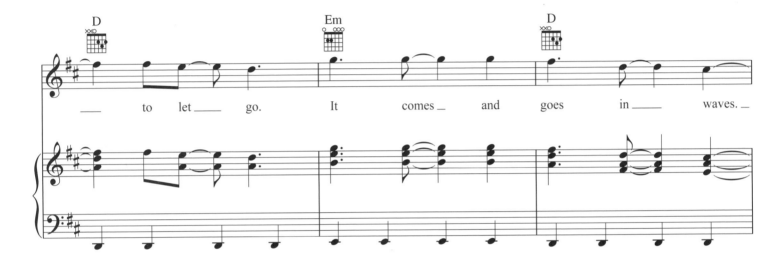

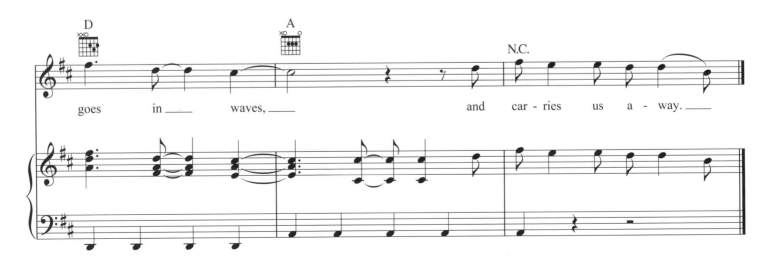

CHEMICALS

Words and Music by
DEAN LEWIS

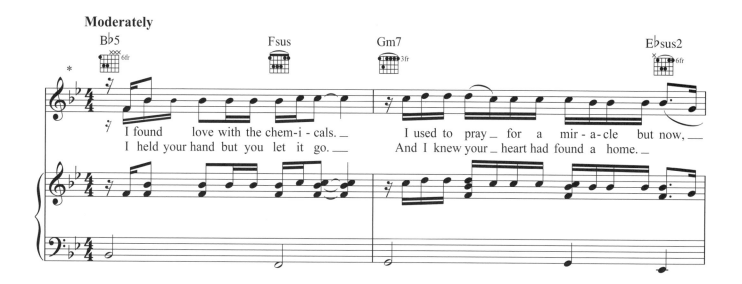

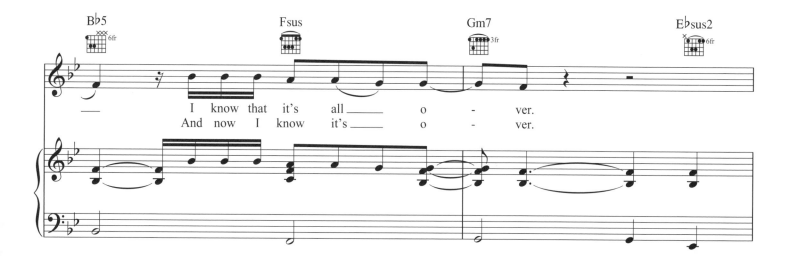

Recorded a half step higher.

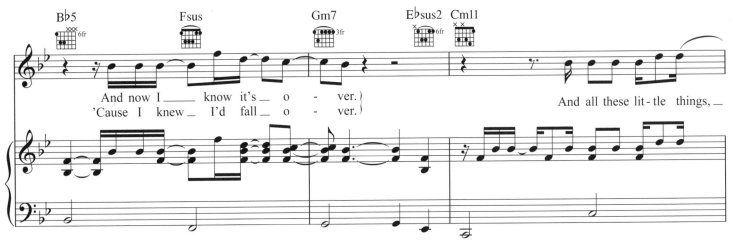

And now I ____ know it's ___ o - ver.
'Cause I knew ___ I'd fall ___ o - ver.

And all these lit - tle things, __

__ they start to slip a - way. __

Hmm, _____ and all these lit - tle things, __

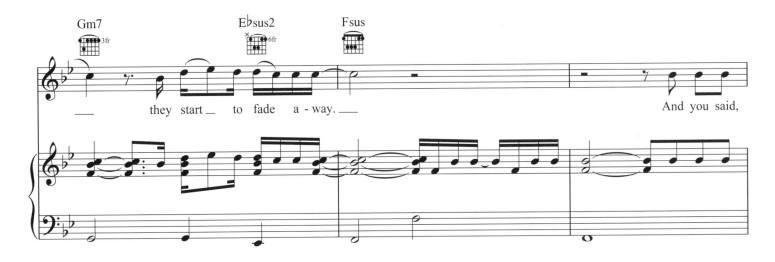

__ they start ___ to fade a - way. __

And you said,

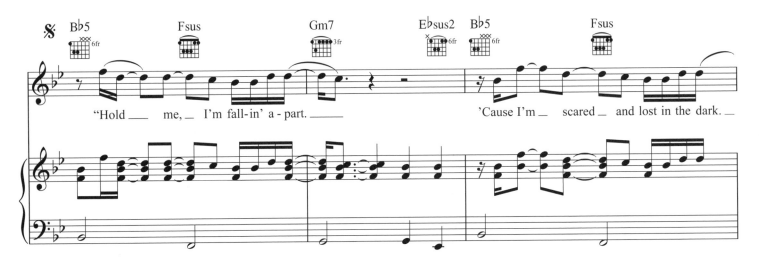

"Hold ___ me, ___ I'm fall-in' a - part. ____

'Cause I'm ___ scared ___ and lost in the dark. __

mak - ing plans __ and break - ing dreams __ when you __ were next __ to me. __

__ It's three A. M. __ in the back of a cab __ and I __ am beg - ging on __ my knees. __

__ Don't go, __ won't __ you stay? I can't stand to watch __ you walk __

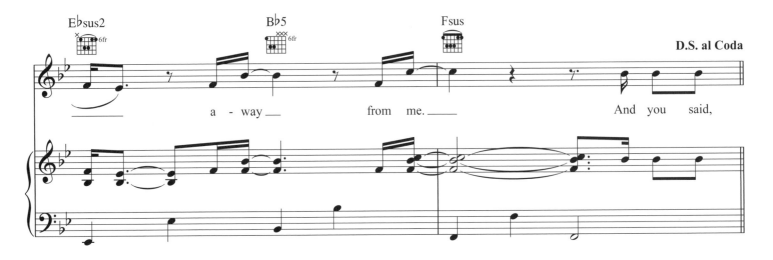

D.S. al Coda

__ a - way __ from me. __ And you said,

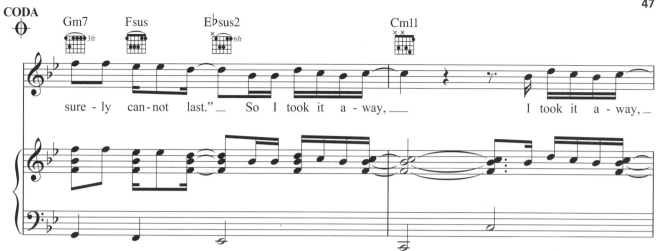

sure - ly can - not last." __ So I took it a - way, __ I took it a - way, __

__ a - way __ from you. __ Hmm, _____

_____ whoa, _____ oh, _____

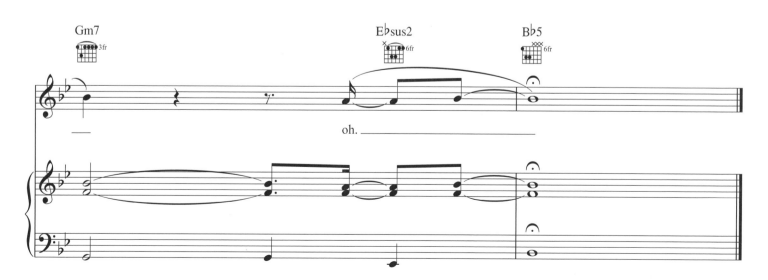

__ oh. _____

BE ALRIGHT

Words and Music by DEAN LEWIS
and JON COBBE HUME

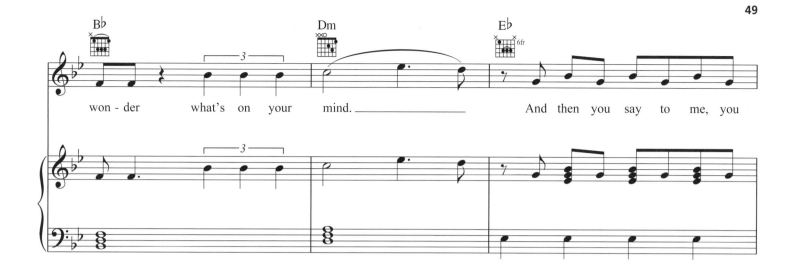

won - der what's on your mind. _____ And then you say to me, you

made a dumb mis - take. You start to trem - ble and your

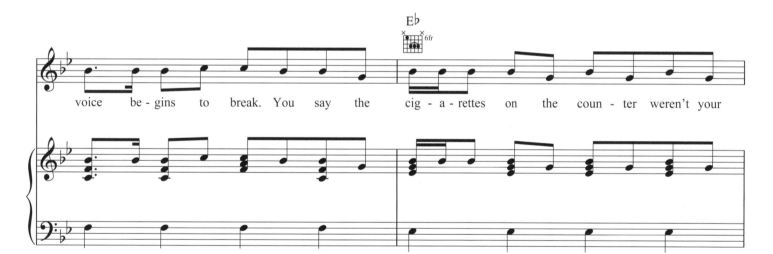

voice be - gins to break. You say the cig - a - rettes on the coun - ter weren't your

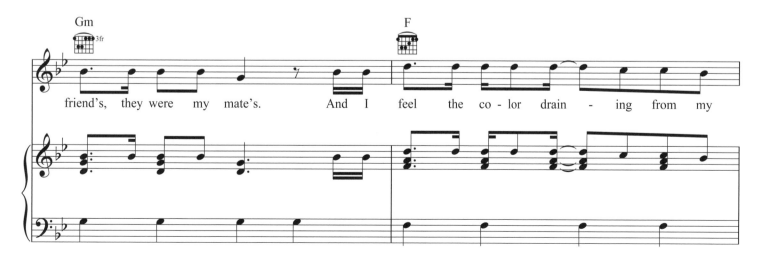

friend's, they were my mate's. And I feel the co - lor drain - ing from my

face. And my friends say: ___ I know you love her, but it's

o - ver, mate. It does-n't mat-ter, put the phone a - way. ___

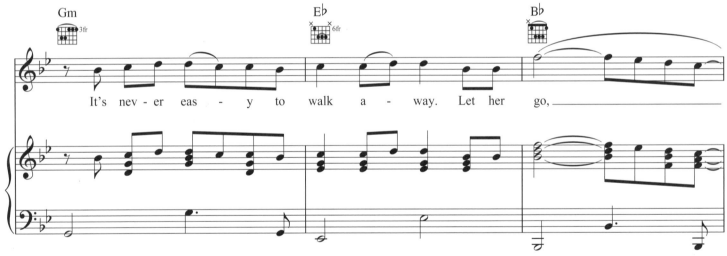

It's nev-er eas-y to walk a - way. Let her go, ___

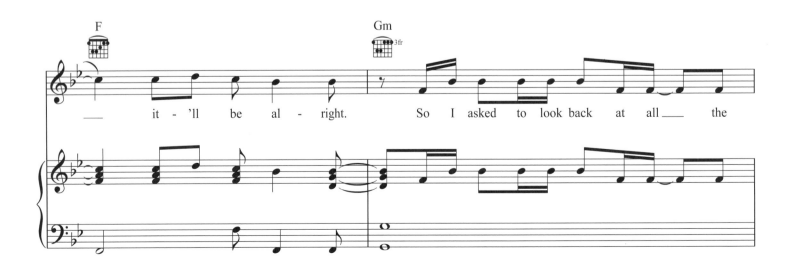

___ it-'ll be al-right. So I asked to look back at all ___ the

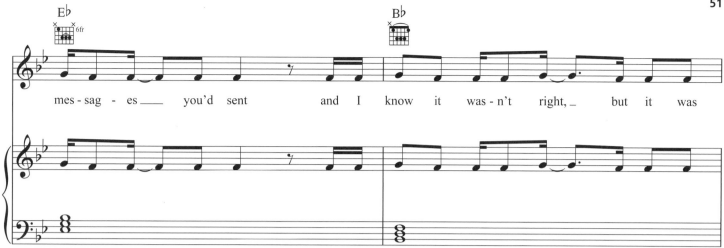

mes - sag - es ___ you'd sent and I know it was - n't right, ___ but it was

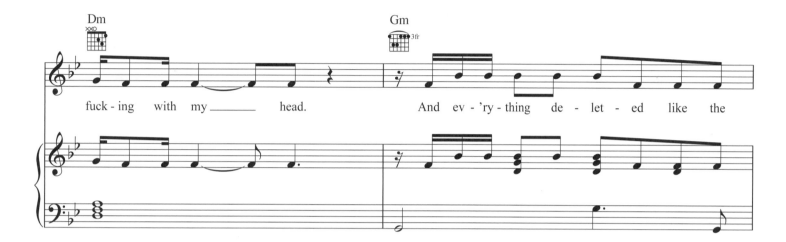

fuck - ing with my ___ head. And ev - 'ry - thing de - let - ed like the

past, yeah it was gone. And when I touched ___ your face, I ___ could

tell you're mov - ing on. But it's not the fact that ___ you

kissed him yes-ter-day, it's the feel-ing of be-tray-al that I

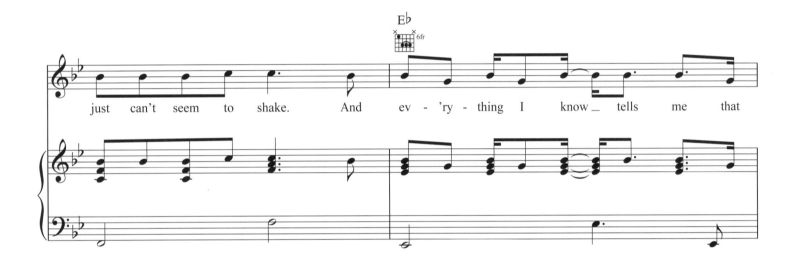

just can't seem to shake. And ev-'ry-thing I know __ tells me that

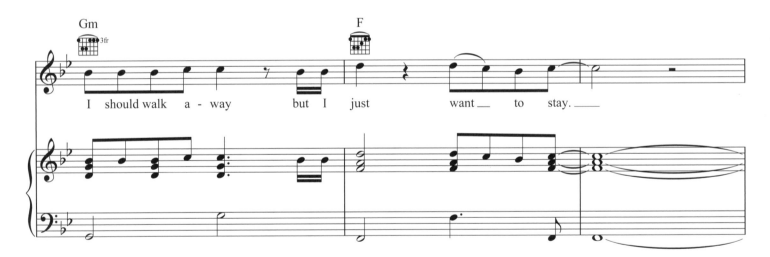

I should walk a-way but I just want __ to stay. __

And my friends say: __ I know you love her, but it's o-ver, mate.

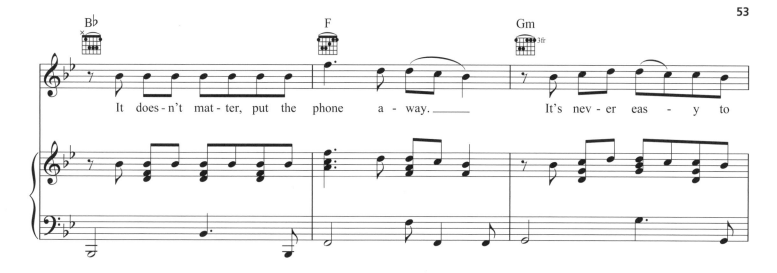

It does-n't mat-ter, put the phone a - way. _____ It's nev-er eas - y to

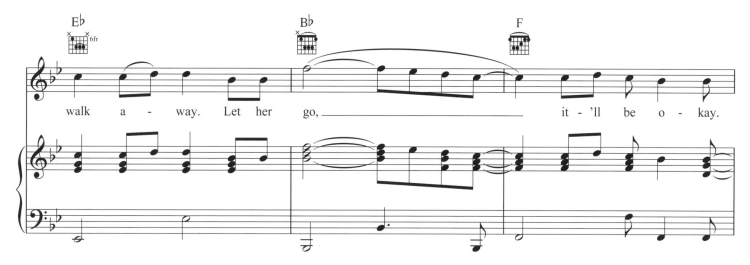

walk a - way. Let her go, _____ it - 'll be o - kay.

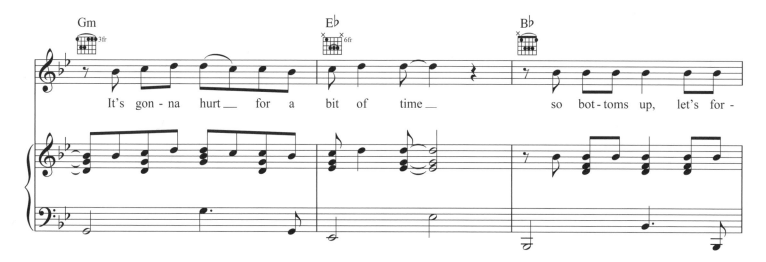

It's gon - na hurt __ for a bit of time __ so bot - toms up, let's for -

get to - night. _____ You'll find an - oth - er and you'll be just fine. __ Let her

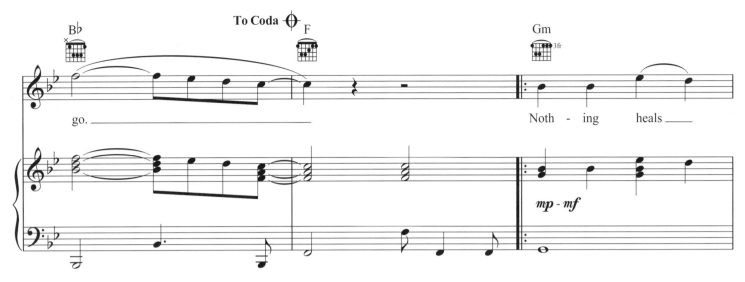

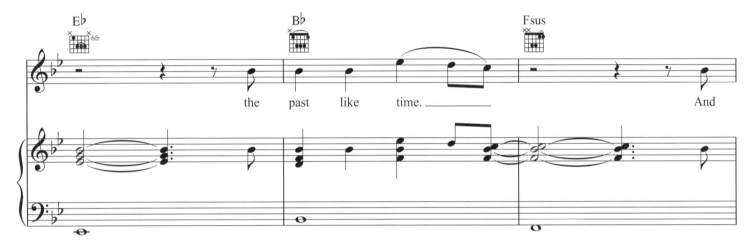

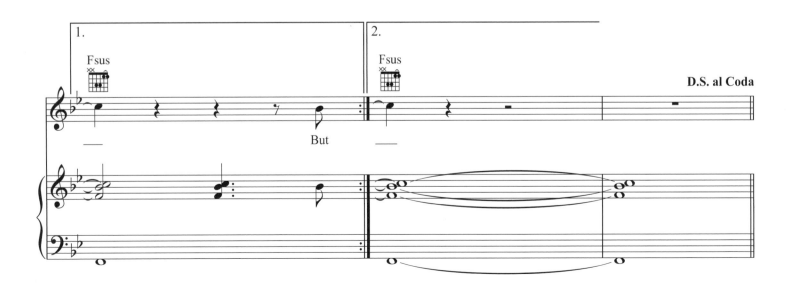

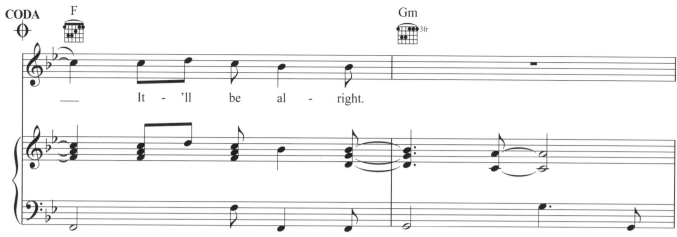

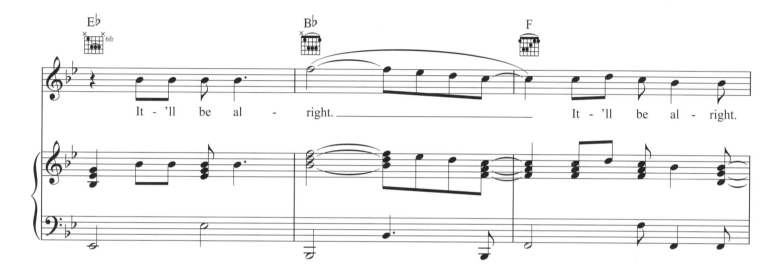

STRAIGHT BACK DOWN

Words and Music by DEAN LEWIS,
NICK ATKINSON and EDD HOLLOWAY

Moderately

mf

With pedal

You know I find it hard to sleep when

I'm sleep-ing by my - self.

And I'm ly-ing in the spare room,

think-ing I should be some - where else.

threw a-gainst the wall. _____ 'Cause we take, _____ and we take just a lit-tle more.

I have no _____ i - de - a what we're fight-ing for. _____ Now I'm stand - ing right

D.S. al Coda

here out-side your door. _____ Now I know, _____ now I know... _____

CODA

wake you up. 'Cause I {can't _____ live with you, _____} I
{Can't _____ live with you, _____}

can't live __ with-out you. You feel __ like home, __ you feel __ like home. _____

And I don't wan-na wake you up, tell you that I'm leav-ing town.

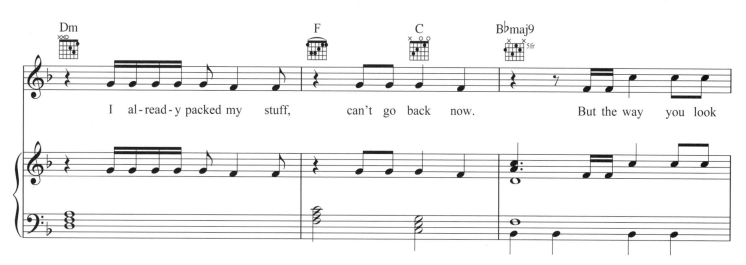

I al-read-y packed my stuff, can't go back now. But the way you look

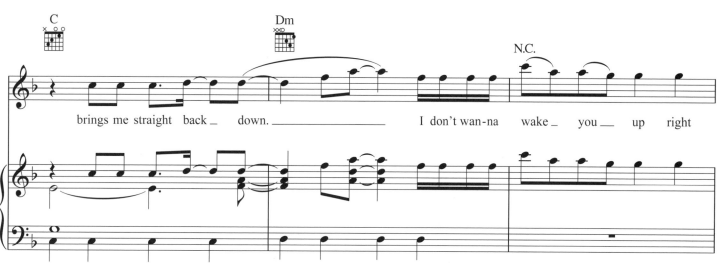

brings me straight back __ down. _____ I don't wan-na wake __ you __ up right

TIME TO GO

Words and Music by
DEAN LEWIS

* Recorded a half step lower.

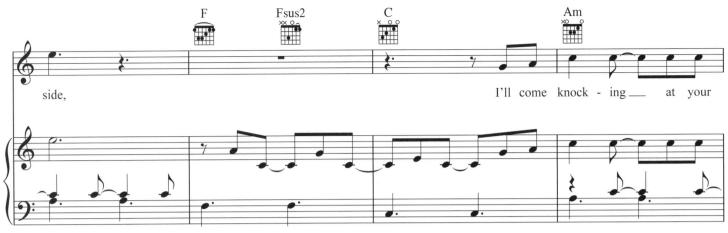

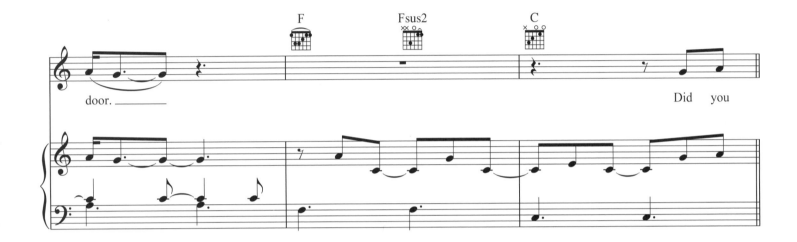

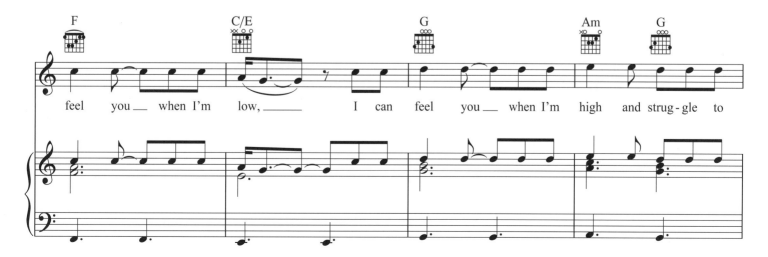

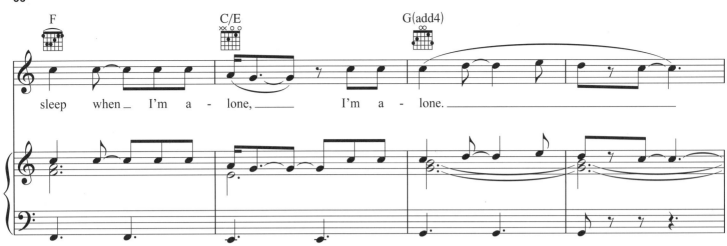

sleep when __ I'm a - lone, _____ I'm a - lone. _____

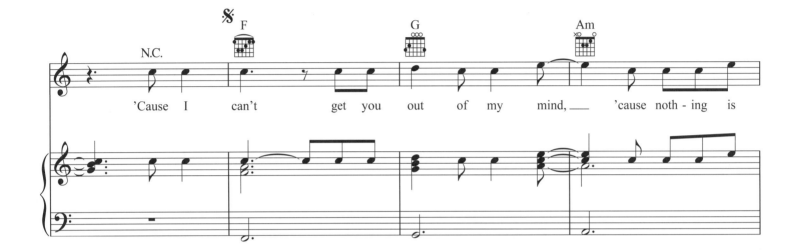

'Cause I can't get you out of my mind, __ 'cause noth - ing is

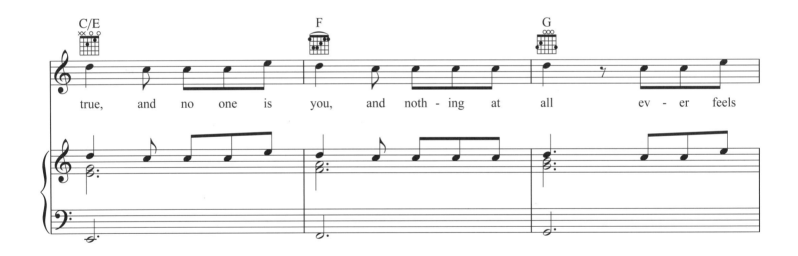

true, and no one is you, and noth - ing at all ev - er feels

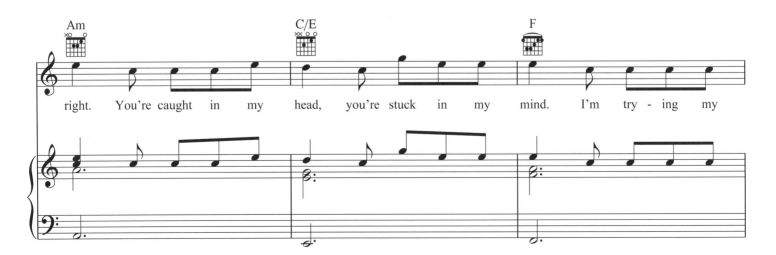

right. You're caught in my head, you're stuck in my mind. I'm try - ing my

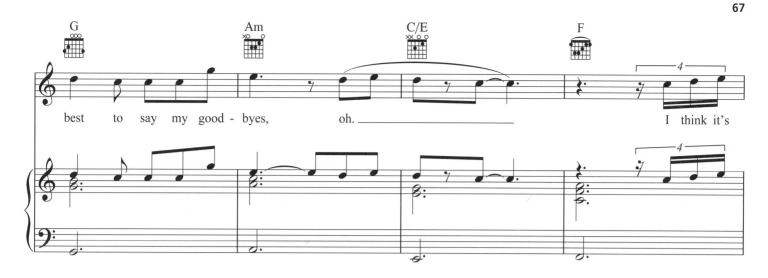

best to say my good - byes, oh. _____ I think it's

time to go. I think it's time to go. _____

It's time to go. _____

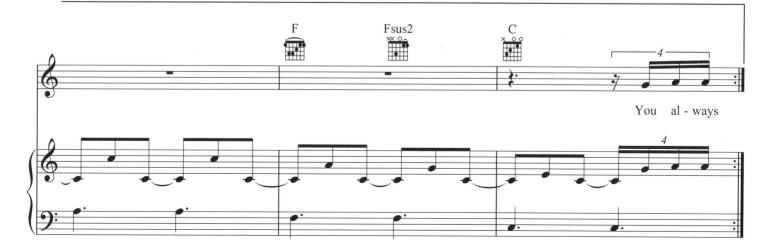

You al - ways

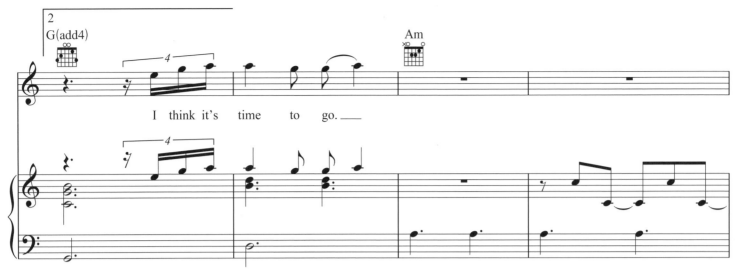

I think it's time to go. ___

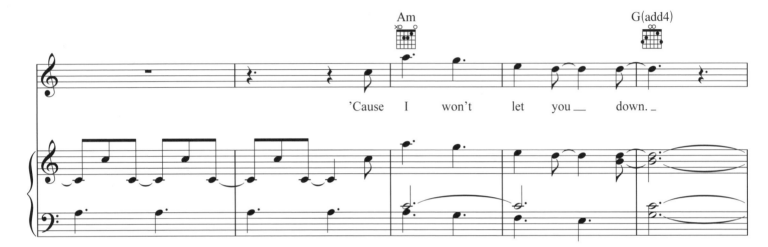

'Cause I won't let you ___ down. _

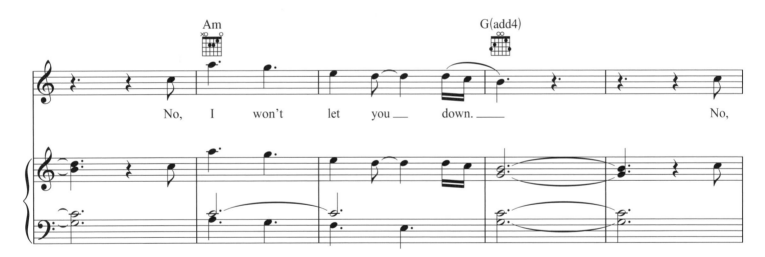

No, I won't let you ___ down. ____ No,

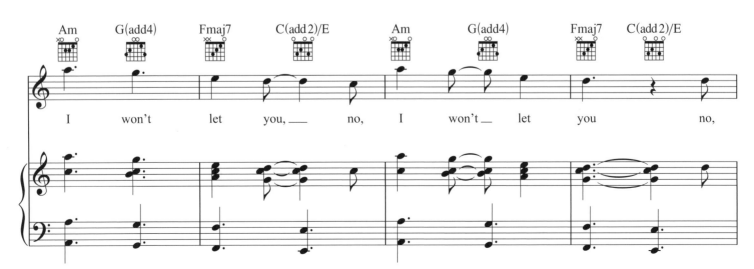

I won't let you, ___ no, I won't ___ let you no,

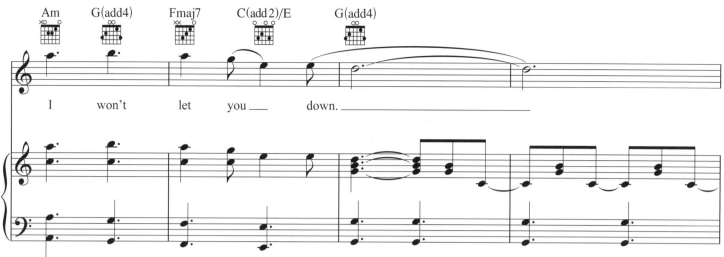

I won't let you ___ down. _____

D.S. al Coda

'Cause I

CODA G(add4)

I think it's

time to go. ___

DON'T HOLD ME

Words and Music by DEAN LEWIS
and JON COBBE HUME

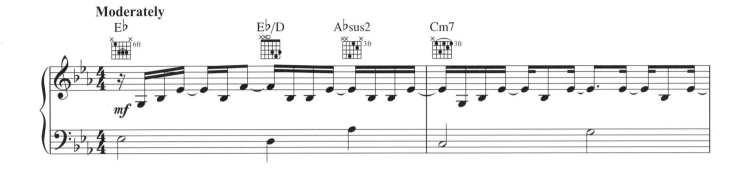

Have you ev-er wished __ you could re-wind __ and

pick up all __ the piec-es of __ the life __ you left be-hind? __

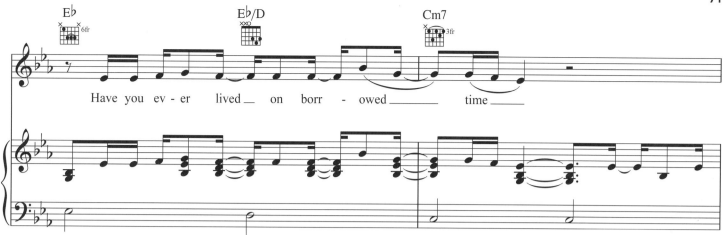

Have you ev-er lived__ on borr-owed_____ time_____

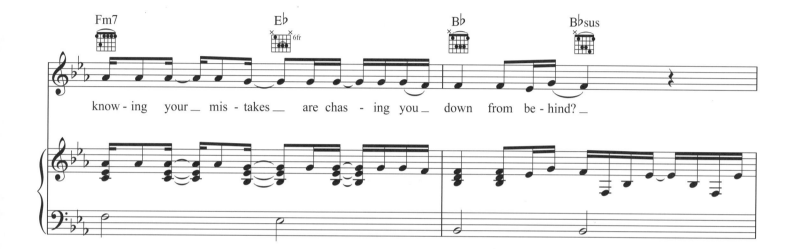

know-ing your__ mis-takes__ are chas-ing you__ down from be-hind? __

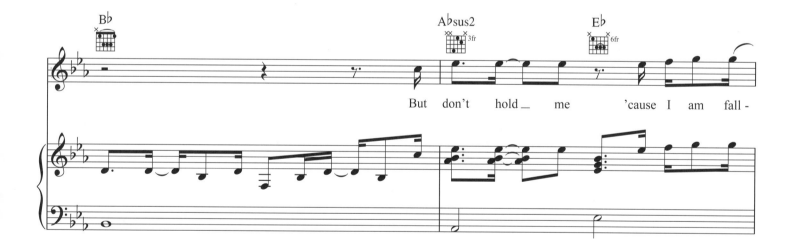

But don't hold__ me 'cause I am fall-

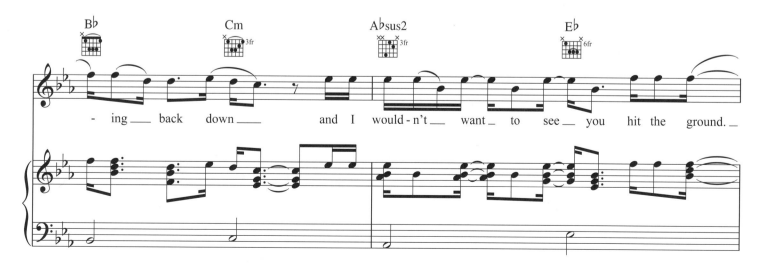

-ing__ back down_____ and I would-n't__ want__ to see__ you hit the ground. __

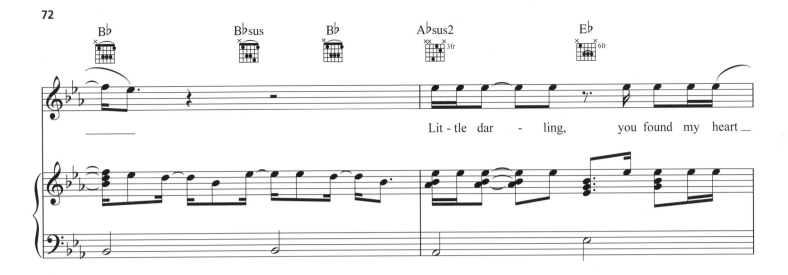

Lit-tle dar - ling, you found my heart

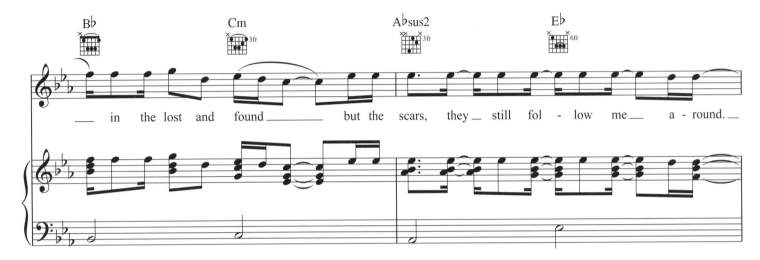

___ in the lost and found ___ but the scars, they __ still fol - low me __ a - round. __

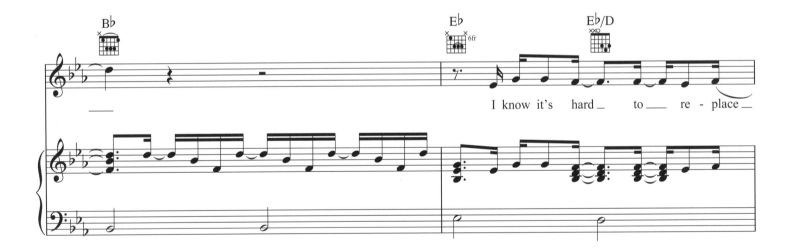

I know it's hard __ to __ re - place __

but the feel - ings that __ you had __ for me __ will one

_____ day be _____ e - rased. _____ And you will learn to _____ move on _____

_____ like foot - prints in _____ the snow _____ are lost _____

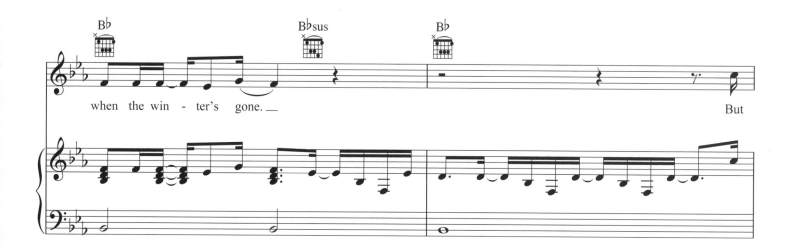

when the win - ter's gone. _____ But

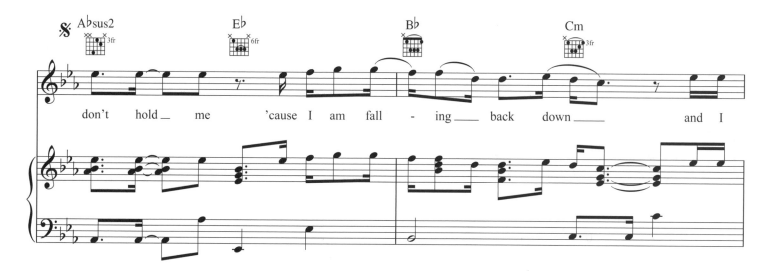

don't hold _____ me 'cause I am fall - ing _____ back down _____ and I

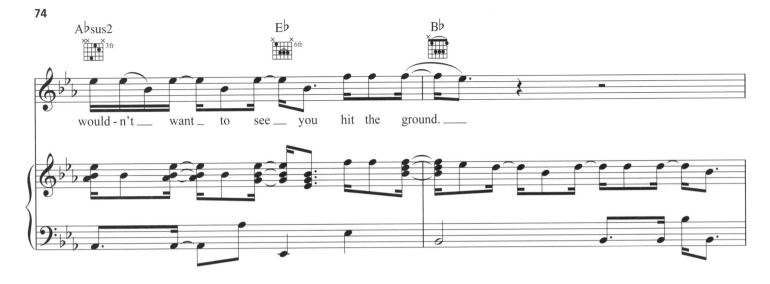

would-n't __ want __ to see __ you hit the ground. __

Lit - tle dar - ling, you found my heart __ in the lost and found _____ but the

scars, they __ still fol - low me __ a - round. __

And the dark __ sur-rounds __ your heart __ and you're in free fall. Oh, you must let __ go ____ of

me. _____ 'Cause if ___ you keep ___ me, you ___ will lose it all. So,

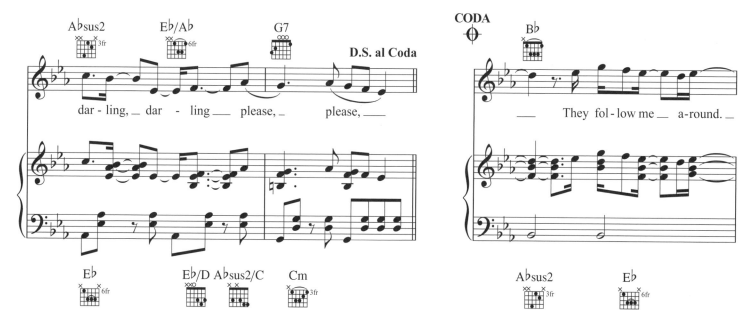

dar - ling, ___ dar - ling ___ please, ___ please, ___

CODA

___ They fol - low me ___ a - round. ___

D.S. al Coda

No, _____

___ they fol - low me a - round. _

FOR THE LAST TIME

Words and Music by
DEAN LEWIS

heard some-bod-y knock-ing at the door, ___ and I
told you to go left ___ and I went right. ___ Though I

had a drink in hand, ___ but I ___ was look-ing for some-thing more. When I ___ put my
told you that I loved ___ you, ___ you could-n't tell ___ that I was ly-ing, 'cause I ___ put a

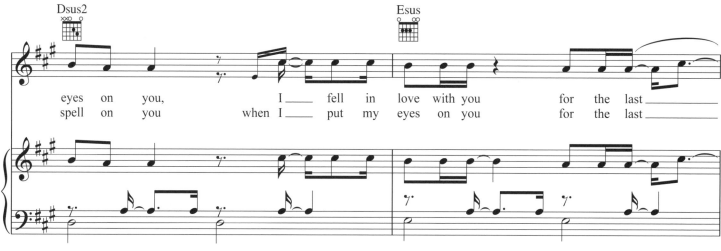

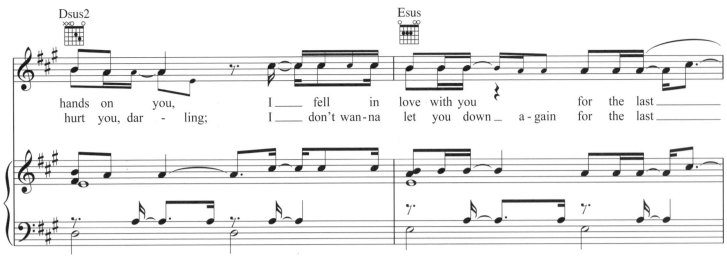

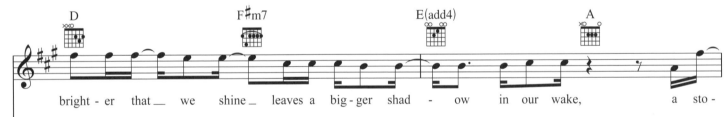

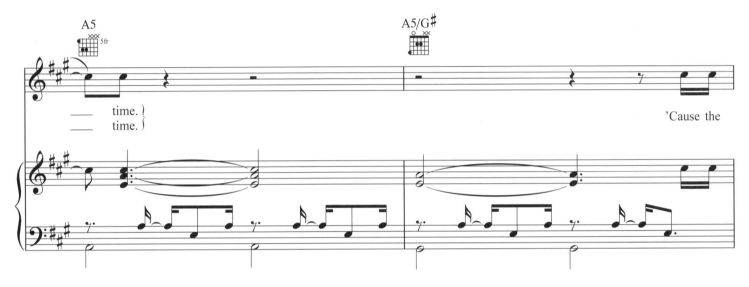

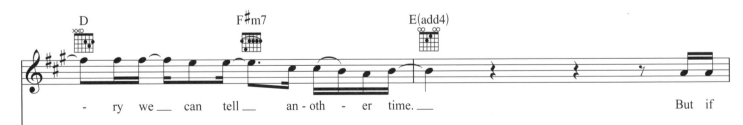

time. ____ But if this was love, __ and I ____ was wrong, ___ then

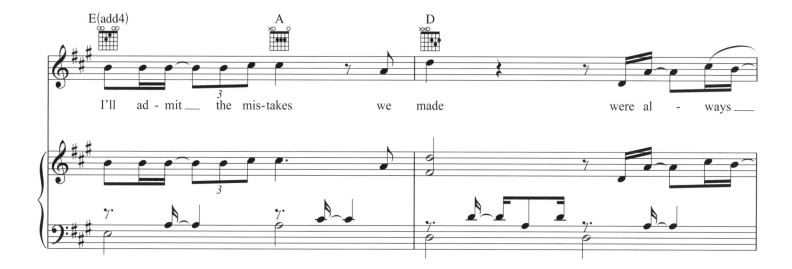

I'll ad - mit ___ the mis-takes we made were al - ways ___

____ mine, were al - ways mine.

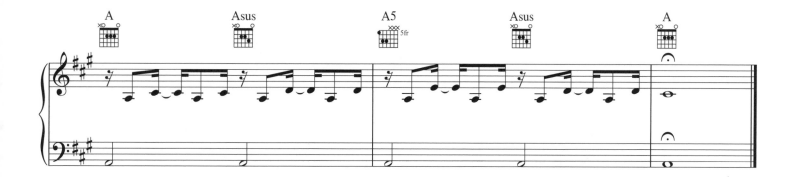

HALF A MAN

Words and Music by DEAN LEWIS,
JON COBBE HUME and HAYLEY WARNER

run - ning from __ my - self, __ 'fraid of what I'd ___ find.

But how am I s'posed to love ___ you when I don't love who I am? _

__ And how can I give you all ___ of me when I'm on - ly half __ a man?

'Cause I'm a sink - ing ship __ that's burn - ing, so let go of my __ hand. _

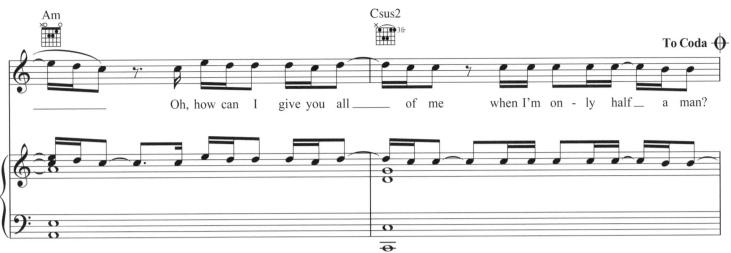

Oh, how can I give you all ____ of me when I'm on - ly half ___ a man?

To Coda

And now I'm stuck in this __ ho - tel __ room by a

cold ne - on light. And I've been wait - ing for an an - swer, but it

won't come _ to - night. And ev - 'ry bot - tle I ___ had sto - len lay

shat-tered on the floor. ___ What's bro-ken can't be whole ___ an-y-

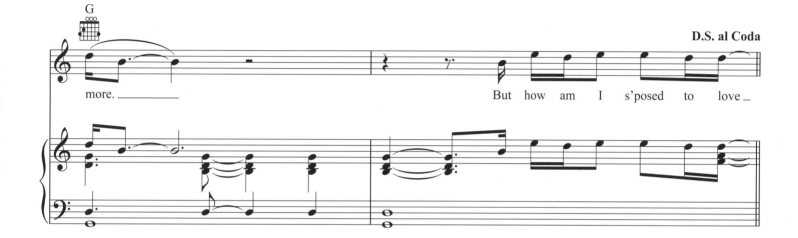

D.S. al Coda

more. ___ But how am I s'posed to love ___

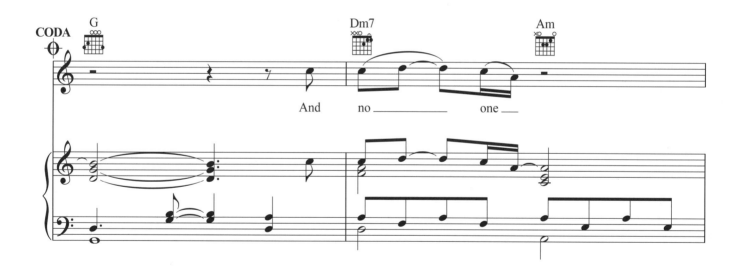

CODA

And no ___ one ___

can ev-er ___ hurt me like I've ___ hurt my-self, ___ 'cause I'm

made out of ___ stone ___ and I'm ___ be - yond ___ help. ___ But

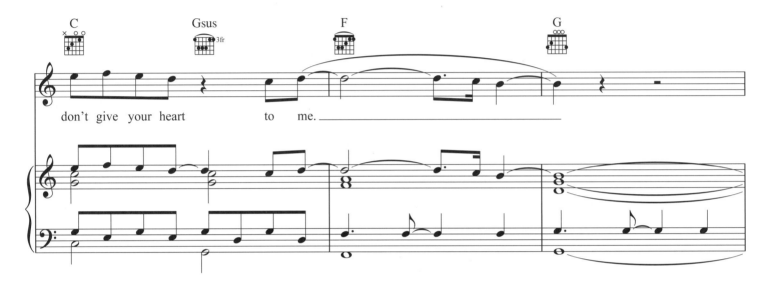

don't give your heart ___ to me. ___

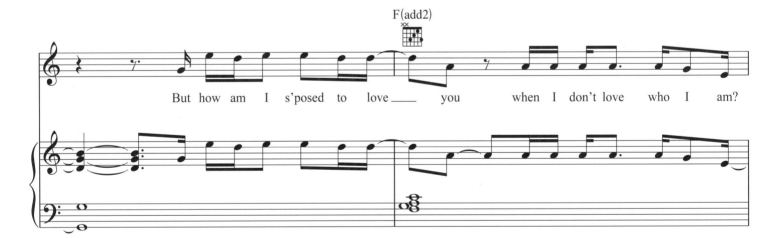

But how am I s'posed to love ___ you when I don't love who I am?

And how can I give you all ___ of me when I'm on - ly half ___ a man?

MORE FROM YOUR FAVORITE ARTISTS

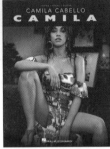

CAMILA CABELLO - CAMILA

All ten tracks from the 2018 debut album by this Fifth Harmony alum which debuted at the top of the Billboard® 200 album charts. Our folio includes piano/vocal/guitar arrangements for the hit single "Havana" plus: All These Years • Consequences • In the Dark • Inside Out • Into It • Never Be the Same • Real Friends • She Loves Control • Something's Gotta Give.
00268761 P/V/G $17.99

ARIANA GRANDE – MY EVERYTHING

This sophomore solo effort from the Nickelodeon TV star turned R&B songstress reached #1 on the Billboard® 200 album charts and has produced several popular hits. A dozen tracks are featured in piano/vocal/guitar arrangements: Be My Baby • Best Mistake • Break Free • Break Your Heart Right Back • Hands on Me • Intro • Just a Little Bit of Your Heart • Love Me Harder • My Everything • One Last Time • Problem • Why Try.
00146042 P/V/G $17.99

NIALL HORAN – FLICKER

This debut solo effort from One Direction's Niall Horan debuted at the top of the Billboard® 200 album charts. Our piano/vocal/guitar folio includes 13 songs from the album: Fire Away • Flicker • Mirrors • On My Own • On the Loose • Paper Houses • Seeing Blind • Since We're Alone • Slow Hands • This Town • The Tide • Too Much to Ask • You and Me.
00255614 P/V/G $17.99

IMAGINE DRAGONS - EVOLVE

This 3rd studio album by Nevada rock band Imagine Dragons was released in the summer of 2017 and reached #2 on the Billboard® 200 album charts. Our matching folio includes piano, vocal & guitar arrangements to the singles "Believer" and "Thunder" as well as 9 moresongs: Dancing in the Dark • I Don't Know Why • I'll Make It Up to You • Mouth of the River • Rise Up • Start Over • Walking the Wire • Whatever It Takes • Yesterday.
00243903 P/V/G $17.99

MAROON 5 - RED PILL BLUES

Maroon 5 keeps churning out the hits with their sixth studio album, this 2017 release led by the single "What Lovers Do" featuring Sza. Our songbooks features piano/vocal/guitar arrangements of this song and 14 more: Best 4 U • Bet My Heart • Closure • Cold • Denim Jacket • Don't Wanna Know • Girls like You • Help Me Out • Lips on You • Plastic Rose • Visions • Wait • Whiskey • Who I Am.
00261247 P/V/G $17.99

P!NK – BEAUTIFUL TRAUMA

This 7th studio album from pop superstar Pink topped the Billboard® 200 album charts upon its release in 2017 led by the single "What About Us." Our matching folio features this song and a dozen more for piano, voice and guitar: Barbies • Beautiful Trauma • Better Life • But We Lost It • For Now • I Am Here • Revenge • Secrets • Whatever You Want • Where We Go • Wild Hearts Can't Be Broken • You Get My Love.
00255621 P/V/G $17.99

ED SHEERAN – DIVIDE

This third studio album release from Ed Sheeran topped the Billboard® 200 album charts upon its March 2017 release, led by the singles "Castle on the Hill" and "Shape of You." Our matching folio includes these two hits, plus 14 others: Barcelona • Dive • Eraser • Galway Girl • Hearts Don't Break Around Here • New Man • Perfect • Save Myself • What Do I Know? • and more.
00233553 P/V/G $17.99

SAM SMITH – THE THRILL OF IT ALL

Smith's sophomore album release in 2017 topped the Billboard® 200 album charts. This matching folio features 14 songs: Baby, You Make Me Crazy • Burning • Him • Midnight Train • No Peace • Nothing Left for You • One Day at a Time • One Last Song • Palace • Pray • Say It First • Scars • The Thrill of It All • Too Good at Goodbyes.
00257746 P/V/G $19.99

TAYLOR SWIFT – REPUTATION

Taylor's 2017 album release continues her chart-topping success, debuting on the Billboard® 200 chart at number 1, led by the first singles "Look What You Made Me Do" and "...Ready for It." Our songbook features these 2 songs plus 13 more arranged for piano and voice with guitar chord frames: Call It What You Want • Dancing with Our Hands Tied • Delicate • Don't Blame Me • Dress • End Game • Getaway Car • Gorgeous • I Did Something Bad • King of My Heart • New Year's Day • So It Goes... • This Is Why We Can't Have Nice Things.
00262694 P/V/G $17.99

HAL•LEONARD®

Contents, prices, and availability subject to change without notice.

For a complete listing of the products we have available, visit us online at **www.halleonard.com**